My mum's got cancer

By Dr Lucy Blunt

Illustrated by Eloise Osborn
her daughter

With an introduction by Petrea King

Jane Curry Publishing

For Peter/Papa and Chloe – whom we love always
Our wonderful extended families – who laughed and cried and looked after babies
Our fabulous friends – who cooked, helped and loved at every turn
Our dedicated and supportive medical teams – for their knowledge and care
For Wendy, Jane and Petrea – who helped our story become a book
And for the other mums, dads, children and families
Who have to be so brave while they walk this road

With our love and thanks
Lucy and Eloise

First published by Jane Curry Publishing
(Wentworth Concepts Pty Ltd)
PO Box 780 Edgecliff NSW 2027
www.janecurrypublishing.com.au

National Library Australia
Cataloguing-in-publication data:

Blunt, Dr Lucy
My Mum's Got Cancer

For children.
ISBN: 978-0-9804758-5-2

Design by Wendy Rapee
wendyr@exemail.com.au
Printed in China by Jade Productions.

Introduction

No parent is ever prepared for a conversation with their child about a diagnosis of cancer. Surely some of the most difficult conversations a parent ever has to initiate revolve around the experience of cancer. How do you tell your child that your life, and indeed your child's world, is about to change dramatically? It can be difficult to know how much to tell and which words to use.

Children are fabulous at overhearing conversations but poor at interpreting what they have heard. They also notice when a conversation stops or is changed when they enter a room. They are acutely aware of the atmosphere at home and if this changes suddenly, and a child is not informed as to the reason, they will often imagine things to be much more serious than if they were given a simple explanation. Indeed, some children feel excluded or not trusted when they sense something is wrong but no one is telling them what has happened. Children don't need to know everything that might happen but they do need to be informed about what has happened and what is being done to help. Some parents hesitate to say the word 'cancer' believing that it will be fearful for the child. It is we parents who are frightened by the word!

Most of us are ill prepared for the kind of conversations that arise when a parent has cancer. We are often so preoccupied with our own fears and concerns that we don't know how and when to initiate a conversation with our children. We are often numb and fearful at the time of diagnosis and we struggle to regain our equilibrium in the midst of this challenging circumstance while juggling appointments, work commitments, family, pets and household responsibilities.

Children at school often say hurtful and untrue things to a child whose parent has cancer. It is not unusual for children to hear, "Everyone who gets cancer dies". This can, quite understandably, alarm a child unnecessarily. Children often act out their fears and concerns indirectly through behaviours such as becoming more clingy, nightmares, bedwetting, temper tantrums or eating or sleeping disturbances. The upset caused by such statements will be greatly lessened if children feel they are being honestly informed of their parent's health situation.

Generally, children over three years of age need to be given information that is suitable for their level of understanding. Older children need to know that there are many different kinds of cancer and different treatments and outcomes.

Children are remarkably adaptable and resilient when they know they will be kept informed. It's good to tell your children, "You might hear all sorts of stories about people with cancer. There are many different kinds of cancer and different treatments depending on what sort of cancer a person has. If you want to know about me and cancer then come and talk to me because I'll always give you honest answers. If I don't know the answer, I'll ask the doctor and let you know."

Lucy and Eloise's book provides a fabulous catalyst for conversations with your children. Children readily relate to Eloise's delightful drawings and may well be stimulated to make their own pictures of their experience. By gently exploring with your children how they feel about you having cancer, you create an honest foundation upon which the bonds of family love and trust are strengthened. Sometimes we don't know how we feel until we hear what we say. Lucy and Eloise have forged a pathway to meaningful conversations between parents and children around the very difficult challenge of living well with — and beyond — cancer.

My daughter and son were seven and four years of age respectively when I was diagnosed with leukaemia nearly twenty five years ago. Initially, I didn't know what to say to my children because I was overwhelmed both with the enormity of the task and the sudden deterioration in my health. This book would have been so helpful to me and my children. My Mum's Got Cancer provides a safe avenue for the gentle conversations of the heart that deepen the bonds of the loving relationship between parent and child.

Petrea King
Quest for Life Foundation
Founder and CEO
www.questforlife.com.au
Author: *You, Me & the Rainbow*,
Rainbow Kids, The Rainbow Garden

Hi my name is Steffie and I have just turned five. I have a baby brother who's one and a half. His name is Toby. He's really cute and he is just learning how to talk. We live with my mum and dad and our floppy-eared rabbit called Fluffy.

My mum has breast cancer. I'm not really sure what that means, but ever since Mum got it, things have really changed.

My mum has always been pretty fit and healthy. She used to go to work for three days a week and on the other days we would stay home together. On those days she would take me and Toby to swimming lessons and do all the jobs that have to be done in the house; like the washing and the cooking and keeping the house tidy (boring!). But when the jobs were finished, we would . . .

go to the park

... or stay at home and build cubby houses under the kitchen table. On Friday afternoons we would go to our friends' houses and have some dinner and a play together.

But then my mum got cancer. She says that it was a big surprise – but not a good surprise, a bad one. She says that she didn't know that she was sick or that she had the cancer inside her body. She says that one day she just found it and when she showed my dad, they both thought that she should go to the doctor.

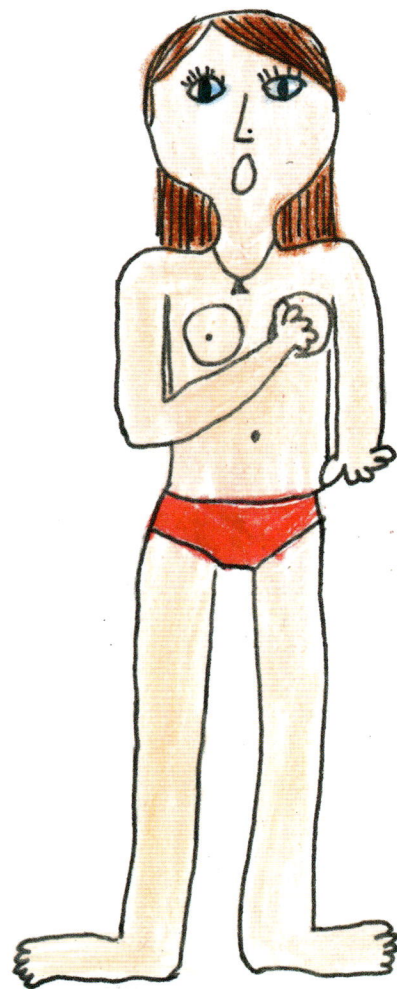

My mum says that she was a bit **frightened** when she went to see our doctor, Dr Gordon, because she was worried about what he was going to say.

She says that he felt the lump in her breast and said that she needed to go and have some special tests done, like x-rays. The tests were to take a picture of what the lump looked like.

My mum says that when Dr Gordon told her that she might have breast cancer, she cried.

Dr Gordon said that our bodies are made up of tiny little cells. These cells need to be healthy and strong so that our bodies can stay healthy and strong.

Dr Gordon said that cancer is a disease which grows inside your body and makes the good healthy cells inside your body become sick. He said that because we have cells all through our bodies, you can get cancer in different parts of the body, not just in the breast.

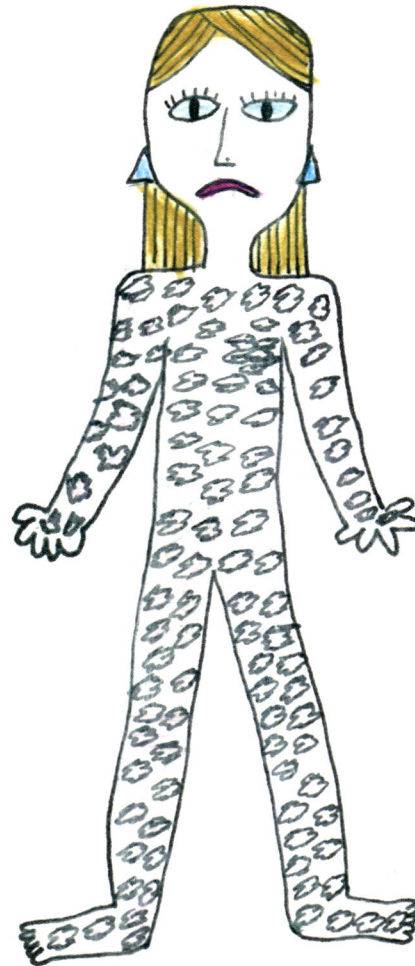

He said that it's nobody's fault if they get cancer, it just happens.

Dr Gordon said that when you have cancer, you have to treat it with really **strong medicine** to stop it from making more of your healthy cells sick.

He said that there were lots of different ways of treating breast cancer and that not everyone would have the same kind of treatment.

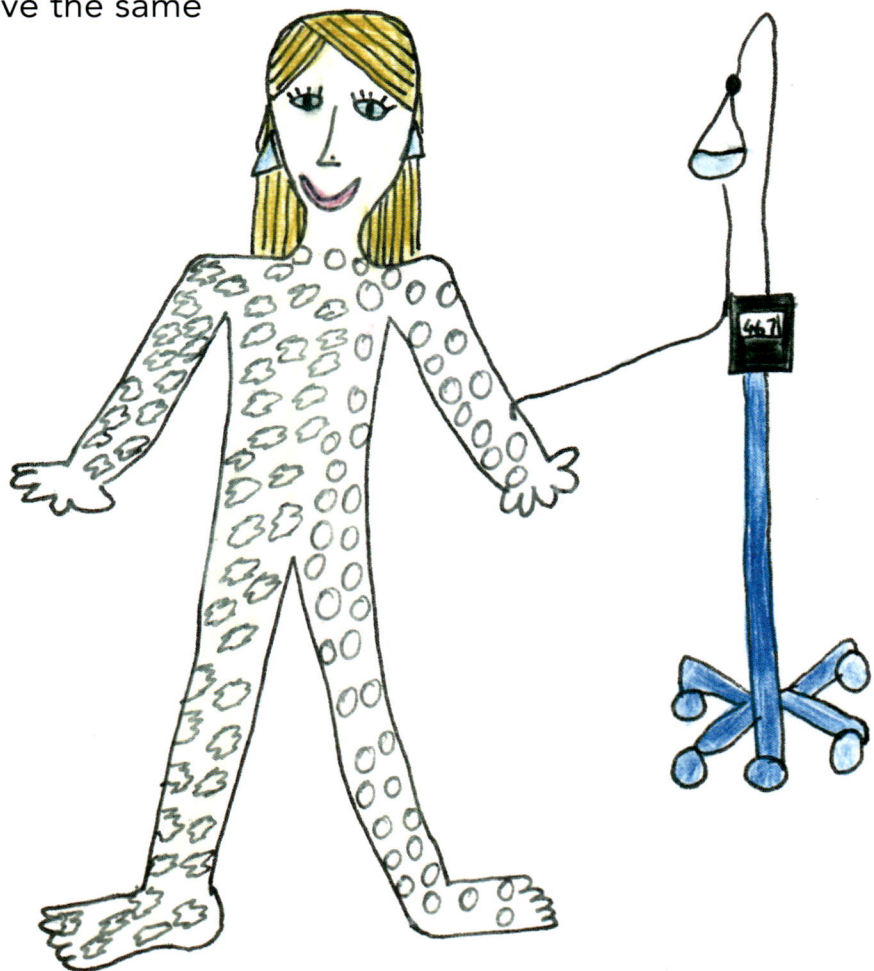

Mum says
that she was worried about
how she was going to look after me
and Toby while she was having the treatment,
because she knew that the strong medicine
would make her feel
sick on some days.

So Mum said that she talked to my dad and her friends about her worries, and they all decided that everyone would help.

She said that she found out that sometimes having a disease like cancer can be a very special thing - because you actually get to see how much people really love you, when otherwise you wouldn't.

Well, let me tell you – my mum must be

really loved!!!!

Over the next few weeks, boy oh boy, everyone showed her how much they loved her. The first thing was the phone didn't stop ringing. It nearly drove us mad!! Lots of our friends and relatives sent flowers and chocolates and books and special things too, until our house looked like a garden.

Then my mum's friends started cooking dinners for us – even my mum's friends' mums cooked food for us! Mum said that our fridge was full of food . . .

. . . and our hearts were full of love.

"Not more spaghetti bolognaise!!"

The operation was to take the lump and some glands underneath her arm out. The operation was done by a surgeon, called Dr Chris.

We went to visit the hospital with Mum before her operation, because she thought it would be a good idea to have a look at where she was going to stay. You should have seen the beds – they were all on wheels!! Toby and I thought they looked really fun. Mum said they were not to play on though, but so that people could be wheeled around the hospital.

We thought that sounded pretty fun too!

We missed Mum when she went to hospital.
We went to see her every day – sometimes
with my grandma or grandpa, sometimes with
my dad and sometimes with our babysitters,
Ann and Sophie.

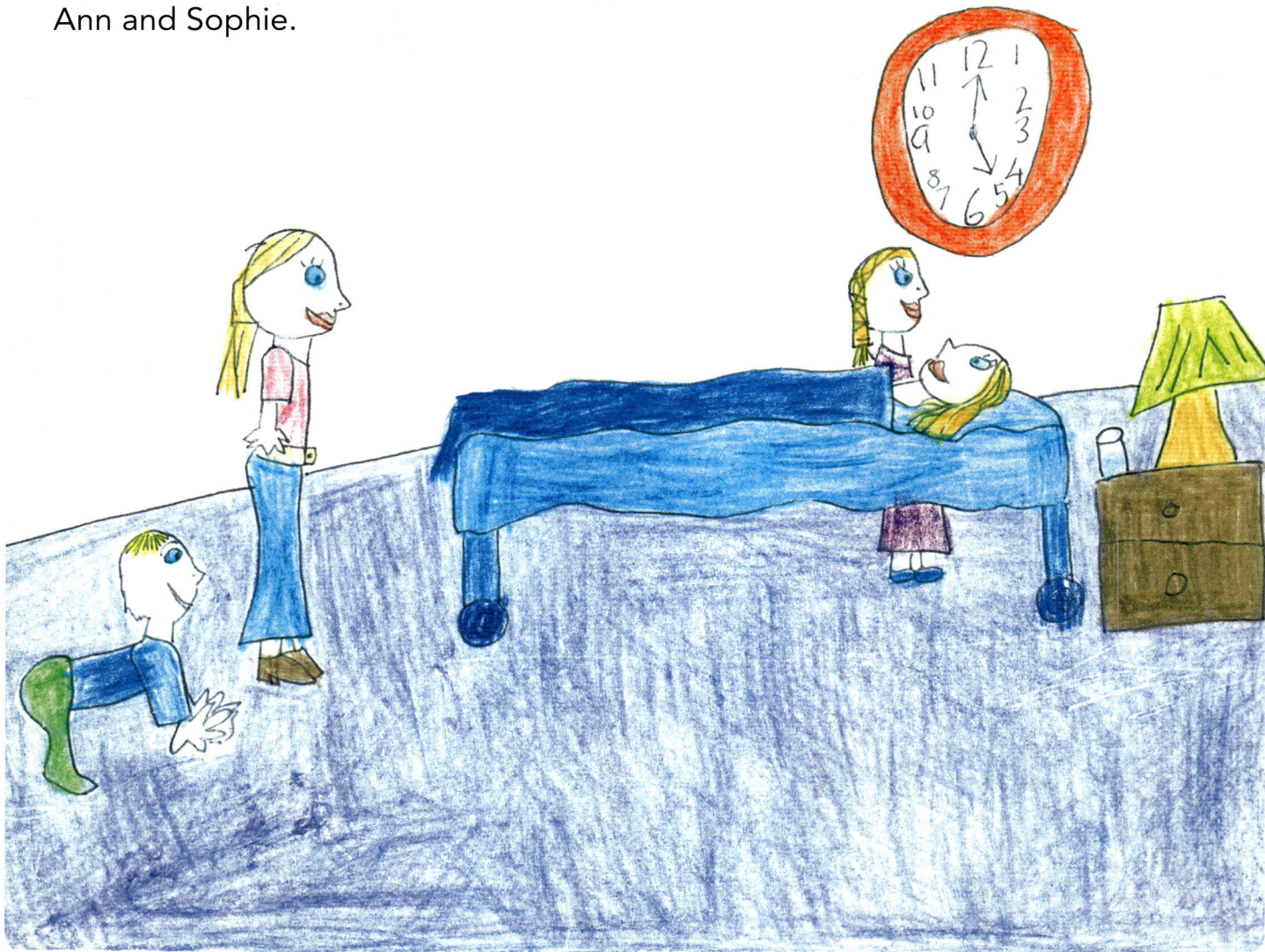

Mum gave us both a little treat every time
we came and said we could open them when
we got back in the car. We felt a little less
sad then because we had something to look
forward to on the way home.

When Mum came home, she was pretty tired and a bit sore. It was great to have her at home and we all started to feel normal again.

... But then she had to start chemotherapy. Mum said that even though Dr Chris had taken the lump of cancer out, chemotherapy and radiotherapy are sometimes used to make sure that there are no leftover bits of cancer in your body.

The chemotherapy was organised by another doctor, called Dr Fran. Chemotherapy is a special medicine that's really strong and powerful. It's strong so that it can fight the cancer cells and make them go away.

The problem is that because it's strong, it can make you feel sick and tired while it's doing the job of killing the cancer cells.

The chemotherapy medicine was so strong though that it made my mum's hair fall out!! Mum was

happy

and said that this was a good sign, as it was meant to happen with her kind of chemotherapy.

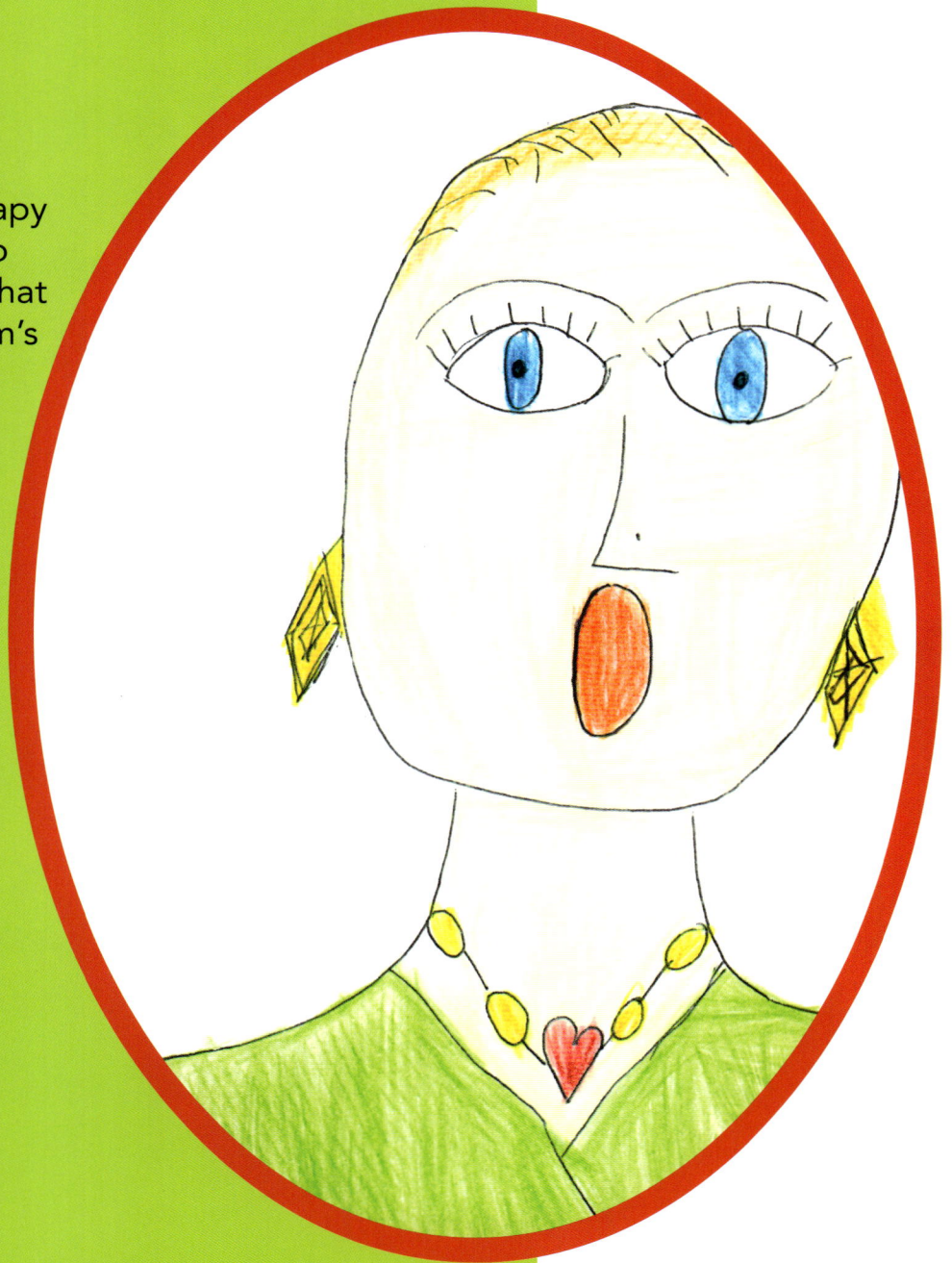

My mum bought lots of funny hats and lots of funny wigs. She would choose which wig she was going to wear depending upon how she was feeling. She had . . .

party hair!

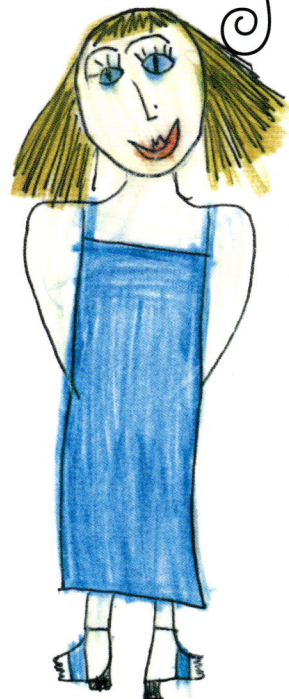

SCARY HAIR!

work hair ...

... and lots of other different wigs too. She and my dad wore different wigs each time they went out to dinner just to make themselves giggle. My mum thought that it was funny and Toby and I did too.

After a while though, I started to get **worried**. Mum was feeling sick a lot of the time and stopped work, because she said she didn't want to work while she wasn't well. My dad or my Aunt Caroline or Uncle George would have to take my mum to the hospital when she had chemotherapy, so that they could drive her home afterwards.

I didn't like my mum going to the hospital to have the chemotherapy, because she would look all right when she went, but she would look different and very sick when she got back. Her face would be red coloured and a bit fatter and she wouldn't smile properly.

I started crying when she went to hospital to have the chemotherapy, because I worried about her. I had secret worries that maybe the cancer cells were getting stronger and that my Mum might die.

When I talked to my Mum about my secret worries, she said that it was just the chemotherapy making her sick, and that she would tell me if the cancer was getting worse. She said that secret worries were much less scary when you talked about them with other people, like your family and your friends.

So my mum spoke to Wendy and Janet, my teachers at pre-school about what we could do. They said Mum should take a camera and take photographs of what happened when she went to hospital. I really liked it when she put all the photos together and made them into a book, because then I could see that nothing really bad had happened, just that she had to have strong medicine.

Mum having a special needle.

Mum saying good-bye to the nurses.

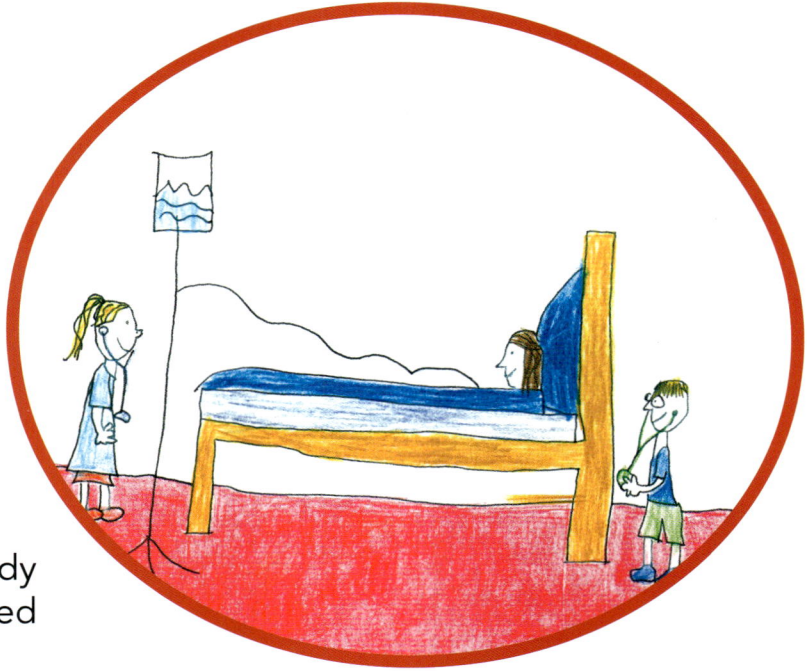

At pre-school, Wendy and Janet also turned a doll's house into a hospital for us to play with and set up **Home corner** with a bed for everyone to lie in when we were pretending to "be sick". We had all kinds of medical equipment too, so we could take turns either being the sick person or else being the doctor.

My mum also goes to see another doctor, Dr Stewart. Mum said that she really likes going to see Dr Stewart, because he is a talking doctor, a psychologist. Mum said that whenever she feels worried, it is good for her to talk about it, so that someone else can help her, just like Wendy and Janet have helped me.

Sometimes my dad goes to see Dr Stewart too. Mum says that it's great to have someone that she and Dad can talk to about all their hopes and fears about her having cancer.

Mum says that there are things that Toby and I do that help her too. She says she loves it when I come home from pre-school and tell her all about my day. She also loves it when we both do drawings or make things for her. Her favourite thing though is when we snuggle up when she's in bed and give her nice big

(cuddles).

Dad does things that help as well. He sends out emails on the computer telling everyone how Mum is, so that she doesn't have to talk on the phone all the time and get too tired.

xox ;)

Now my mum has stopped chemotherapy and is doing **radiotherapy**. She has been doing it for a while now, and guess what? Her hair is growing back!!

She says that now that she has finished taking the chemotherapy, her hair can grow back and she can start feeling better again.

The chemotherapy is still fighting the cancer inside her body, but she doesn't have to take any more.

My mum's radiotherapy doctor is called Dr Rebecca. Mum has to go to radiotherapy from Monday to Friday every day for 6 weeks. Mum doesn't mind the radiotherapy and says that it is good to be doing everything that she can to help fight the cancer.

Toby and I go to the radiotherapy centre sometimes. My grandma or grandpa or our family friends take us to the hospital with Mum, because she still gets a bit

tired.

The radiotherapy doesn't take very long to do, and we are allowed to watch her on the television while they do the special treatment with her. We sit and talk to our friends or read books while Mum has her treatment or else watch her on the screen with the people who work there.

H

party!

H=HAIR, HEALTH, HAPPINESS

Mum's treatment is taking a **looooooong** time. I am nearly 6 now and Toby has already turned 2!!! My mum says that when she finishes all of her treatment, that she is going to have an "H" party. All our friends are going to come wearing their favourite wigs. Mine is a black one with plaits all over it and beads on the bottom. We're going to dance to disco songs and celebrate my mum being well again.

My mum says that life is going to get back to normal again soon. She will cook our family dinners herself, go back to work, pick me up from pre-school and take me to swimming lessons again . . . it will just be her and Toby and me going to the park, with no one else. She says that she will get healthy and strong again and take some medicine every day to stay well . . .

. . . but the absolutely best part about finishing treatment though, will be that she can go back to just being my mum.